The Superhero Brain

Christel Land

Illustrated by Shanaka Thisara

ISBN-13: 978-1542887212
ISBN-10: 1542887216

To Kian, with love

In every head there is a brain
But no two brains are alike.

It makes the world an amazing place
When there's something special in every face.

There's one kind of brain called 'the autistic brain',
But that's a bit of a funny name.

I like to call it the superhero brain instead,
Because it means you have superpowers inside your head!

The superhero brain can hear things that a lot of people miss.

Like the littlest noise in the grass from a toad,
Or a car starting its engine far down the road.

The superhero brain can feel things that a lot of people miss.

Like a tickly tag inside your clothes,
Or the rumbling in the ground when a train sets off and goes.

The superhero brain can taste things that a lot of people miss.

Like every little part of the tastiest fruit,
Or how a snack tastes differently if you eat it on a bus route.

The superhero brain can smell things that a lot of people miss.

Like someone's smelly toes in the next room,
Or a flower in the garden getting ready to bloom.

The superhero brain can see things that a lot of people miss.

Like the tiniest star on a sparkling sky,
Or the fluttering wings of a dragonfly.

The superhero brain can think and create
In ways that are truly amazing.

The most beautiful music in the world,
The most brilliant buildings
And the fastest train.

Lots of them were made by a superhero brain.

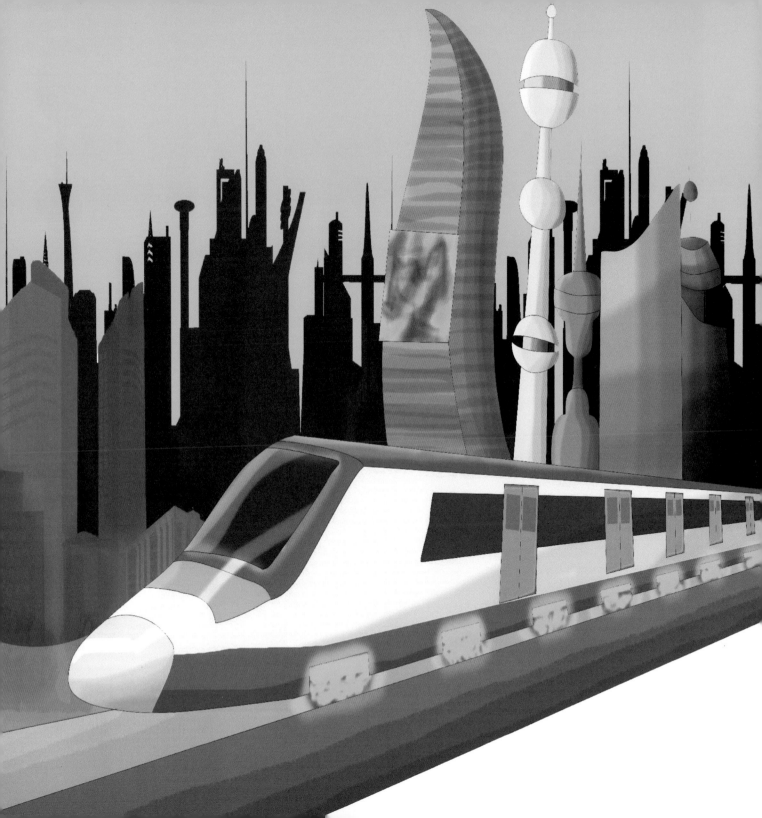

When something feels exciting
It's almost too much to bear.

The hands can flap, the legs can jump
There's something happening everywhere!

It might feel tricky to fall asleep at night,
Because all that superheroing can make your body feel bright.

But all these special powers do make you feel a little tired.
The superhero needs to be alone and rest to get inspired.

Sometimes the world doesn't understand these special brains
And it can feel like a confusing space.
That's when it's time to go to your calm, quiet place.

That place is peaceful, safe, quiet and warm too
And it sits deep inside you.

Take a breath, close your eyes
Remember a picture of clear, blue skies.

Let the calm fill you from the inside, all the way out
Until your mind is free of any doubt.

Some people call it 'finding your zen'
All it means is, you're ready for the world again.

And if you feel like you can't find that place on your own
Come and find us, you're never alone!

We will help you work things out
Because that is what loving you is really about.

So if you have a superhero brain
Work out what amazing things your brain can do.
Then go and use your special powers
To do incredible things, you too!

Whatever road your life may go
Let your superhero brain help you glow.

Find things that make you smile,
Find things that you can put in rows or pile.

Find ways to fix important problems,
Find ways to make your spirit blossom.

Once you know what you can do,
Go out and do it!
Your dreams can come true!

The first time someone told me about my superhero brain was this day:

And these are our memories from that day:

Have you met the superhero heart?

"If someone you know has
a superhero brain,
You'll know already there's more than one
way to be smart.

And maybe no one told you,
But it also means you have a
superhero heart!"

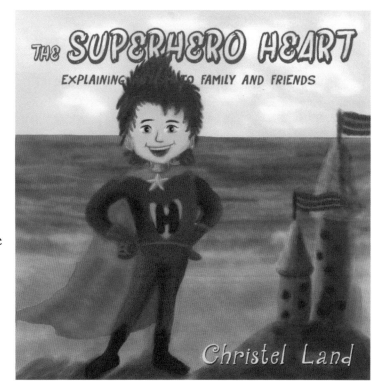

To help your child relate to the story, each book is available with a number of different characters.

One of our readers has developed a tool of her own
to build confidence in kids.
A star of positive affirmations that your child
can read to him/herself!

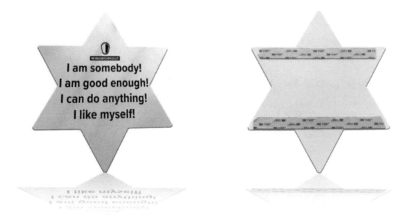

http://affirmationstar.myshopify.com

Printed in Great Britain
by Amazon